Antonia Novello
Doctor

Written by Mayra Fernández
Illustrated by Rick Villarreal

MODERN CURRICULUM PRESS

Program Reviewers

Anna M. López, Director,
   Bilingual Education and Foreign
   Languages
   Perth Amboy Public Schools
   Perth Amboy, New Jersey

Kerima Swarz, Instructional Support
   Teacher
   Philadelphia School District
   Philadelphia, Pennsylvania

Eva Teagarden, Bilingual Resource
   Specialist
   Yuba City Unified School District
   Yuba City, California

Gladys White, Bilingual Program
   Manager
   East Baton Rouge Parish School
   Board
   Baton Rouge, Louisiana

MODERN CURRICULUM PRESS

13900 Prospect Road, Cleveland, Ohio 44136

A Paramount Publishing Company

Copyright © 1994 Modern Curriculum Press, Inc.

ISBN 0-8136-5268-5 (Reinforced Binding)   0-8136-5274-X (Paperback)

Library of Congress Catalog Card Number: 93-79436

Dear Readers,

In this book you will meet a person who did two "firsts" at the same time—Antonia Novello became the first Hispanic Surgeon General and the first woman Surgeon General. Once it seemed this sickly little girl couldn't have her dream of being a doctor. But she kept dreaming, reading, and studying.

You, too, can have your dream. Follow Antonia's example. Keep your dream and then do it. Antonia would be the first to say, "Yes, you can!"

Your friend,

Mayra Fernández

Antonia, the oldest child of Antonio and Ana Coello, had always dreamed of being a doctor. For a girl born in 1944 with poor health, that was a very big dream.

Antonia, who lived on the island of Puerto Rico, spent most of her childhood summers in the hospital. She had been born with a problem with her intestines. This made it difficult for her to digest food on her own. At the hospital, doctors and machines helped Antonia's body correct this problem.

3

4

Antonia always hoped her visits
to the hospital would not last too
long. But she never spent less
than two weeks there.

Each time she had to go she
would pick up her teddy bear
and take her mother's hand. Her
mother always made Antonia feel
special and loved.

The hospital was like a second
home to Antonia. The nurses and
the doctors were her special buddies.
Here, Antonia thought more about
being a doctor. She did not tell
anyone, not even her mother, about
her dream.

6

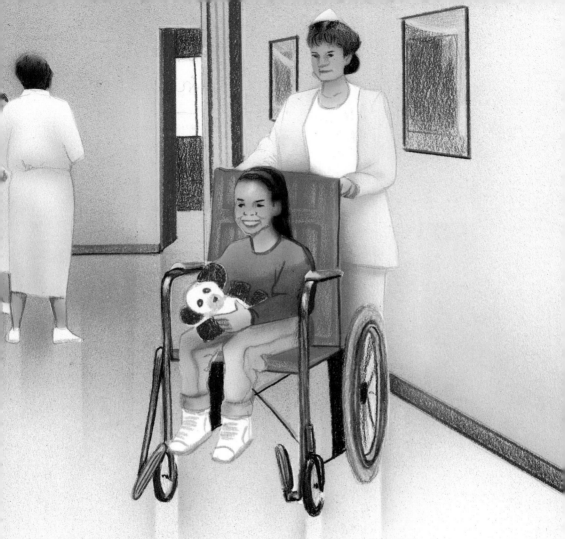

Antonia was not sure she could
become a doctor. She knew that to
become a doctor she would have to
work hard. Because of her sickness,
she was not very strong.

7

8

Antonia's mother had been told that
Antonia would need an operation
some time. But she tried to make
Antonia's childhood as much like
other children's as she could.

In 1952, when Antonia was eight
years old, a very sad thing happened
in the Coello family. Antonia's
father died.

When she was 18, Antonia had the
operation she needed. Soon afterward,
she went to college even though she
was not completely healed.

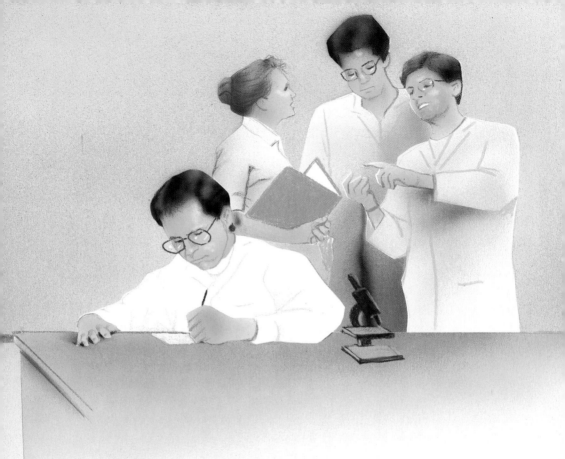

Antonia knew then that if she had the courage to go to college while still recovering from her operation, she could do anything! She could be a doctor.

Antonia was very proud to be one of only 65 students accepted to the University of Puerto Rico Medical School. She finished medical school in 1970.

Antonia became a pediatrician—a doctor who cares for children. She knew what sick children go through. Antonia even gave some children teddy bears just like the one she had owned.

In the same year Antonia became a doctor, she married Joseph Novello, a doctor for the Navy. They lived in Springfield, Virginia. There Antonia helped many sick children.

In 1978, she took a job with the National Institute of Health. She worked especially hard to help children with kidney problems. A few years later, she was put in charge of other doctors.

Because of her hard work, Antonia was named to her most important job yet. On March 9, 1990, she was named Surgeon General of the United States. She became the doctor for all Americans, the person who gives advice to the President on public health problems.

Antonia was the first woman and the first Puerto Rican to have this job. Her mother was very proud and stood next to Antonia when she was sworn in.

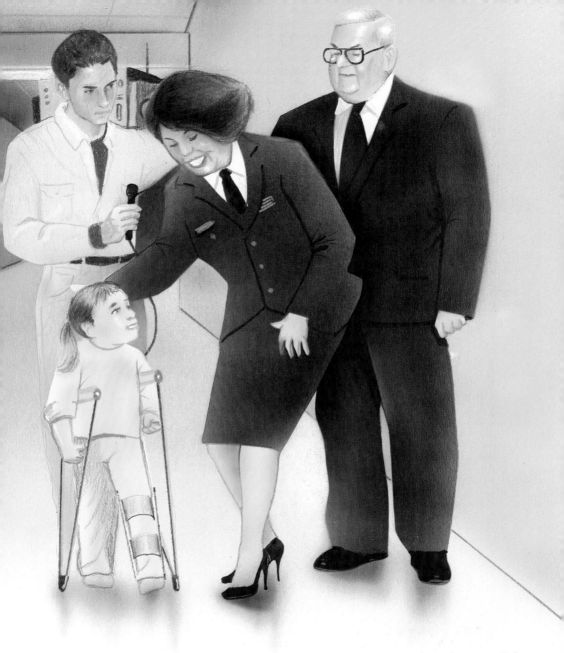

Antonia made sure people worked on curing AIDS and other diseases. She realized many children were dying from measles. So she tried to help poor mothers get measles shots for their children. She also tried to help people who were sick because they drank too much alcohol. These are only a few of the problems she tried to help with.

23

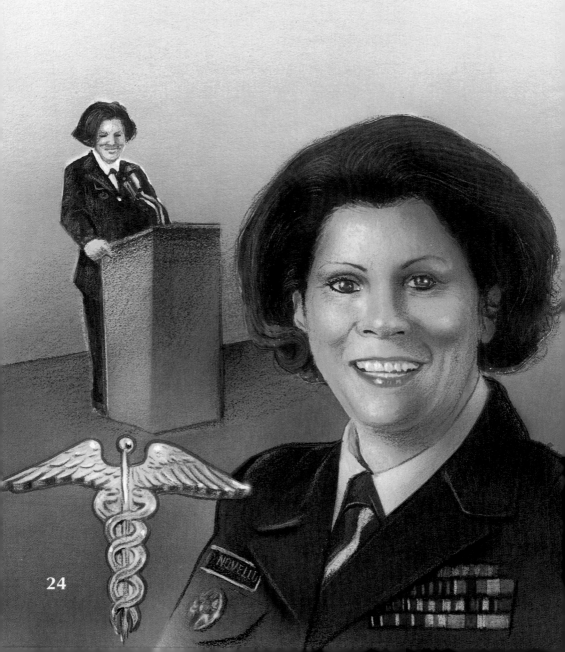

24

One day Antonia received
a letter from a nine-year-old
girl who wrote, "I'm intelligent,
and I want to meet you
because I'm going to be the
second woman Surgeon
General."

Antonia knew that, thanks
to what she had done, this little
girl had the courage to follow
her dream. This young girl
could become a doctor, or an
astronaut, or anything else she
wanted to be.

Glossary

AIDS (ādz) Acquired Immune Deficiency Syndrome, a virus that attacks the immune system of the patient. To this day it is fatal.

alcohol (al' kə hôl) A drug that becomes habit-forming and causes sickness in people who drink too much of it

pediatrician (pē' dē ə trish' ən) A doctor for children

Puerto Rico (pwer' tō rē' kō) An island in the Caribbean. It is a part of the United States, officially called the Commonwealth of Puerto Rico. It has its own governor and its own flag. The people born there are U.S. citizens.

Surgeon General (sur' jən jen' ər əl) The person who advises the President on public health problems. The office of the Surgeon General is part of the U.S. Department of Health and Human Services.

About the Author

Mayra Fernández is a teacher in East Los Angeles, California. Dr. Fernández has been teaching for 27 years. She has twelve children, six of whom are adopted. Three of the adopted children are Mexican-American, one is Cuban, one Nicaraguan, and one Pakistani. All form a rainbow of love around her life. Dr. Fernández is kept busy teaching, writing poetry and stories, and giving workshops to parents and teachers. She dedicates this book to Greg, one of her rainbow children.

About the Illustrator

Rick Villarreal completes his training in illustration and fine arts at Chicago's Academy of Art this year, but he has already begun his career as a commercial illustrator with nationally known businesses and has provided caricatures for area newspapers. Although he especially likes sports themes, he also hopes to illustrate movie posters and video game covers. In *Antonia Novello*, he has worked in his favorite medium, air brush, with detail added in colored pencil.